Animals on the Farm
A Dog Named Rooster

Lucy M Johnson, PhD

COPYRIGHT

Copyright 2024 © Lucy M. Johnson, PhD

All rights reserved. No part of this book may be used or reproduced in any manner whatsoever without the prior written permission of the author.

ISBN:

978-1-962911-06-01

DEDICATION

To the Farmer who built and maintains the farm. It is here where all the farm adventures are made. Thank you for all your hard work and dedication that you continuously provide to your family and all the farm animals who call Horseshoe Ridge Farms & AirBnB their home.

ACKNOWLEDGEMENTS

Thanks to God for providing the farm where we make many wonderful family memories; my inspirational place, my paradise, where the Animals on the Farm series takes place.

Thanks to my mother who has always continued to inspire me from heaven above.

Thanks to the Farmer, my husband, who has supported me throughout the decades in all my personal and professional adventures, and who assisted me with editing this book.

One bright and sunny day a farmer and his wife drove from their farm in West Virginia to another farm in Virginia.

They were very excited to take this trip as they were going there to see their farmer friends in Virginia and pick up their new puppy.

This puppy would not be just any ordinary puppy.

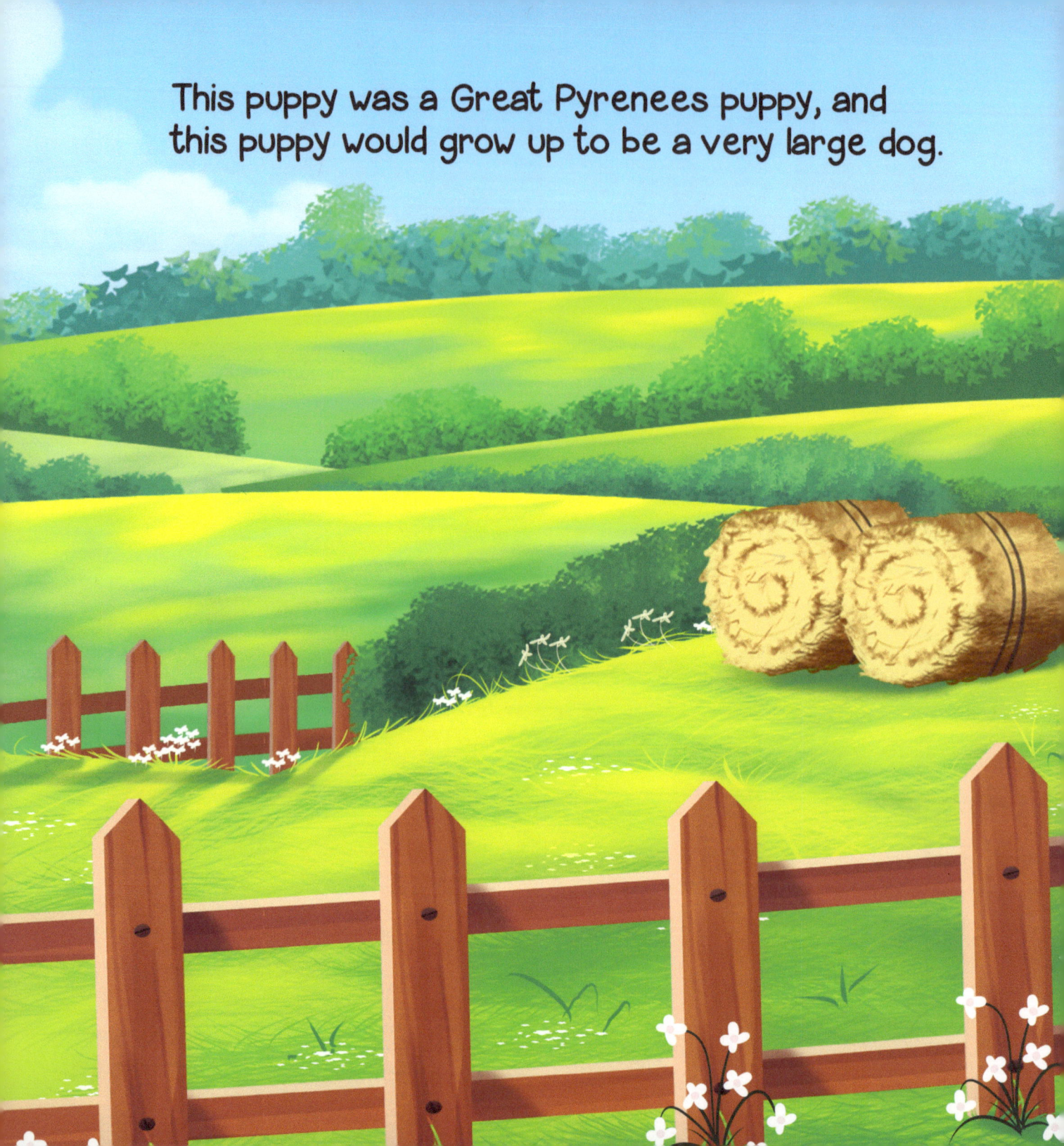

This puppy was a Great Pyrenees puppy, and this puppy would grow up to be a very large dog.

This puppy would become a working dog at Horseshoe Ridge Farms. Did you know that dogs can have jobs?

Hiring Working Dogs

The job this puppy would do when he was big enough, would be protecting livestock on the farm.

You see, Great Pyrenees dogs are livestock protectors, and this puppy was being "hired" to be a protector!

Great Pyrenees dogs sleep a lot during the daytime and stay awake at night to guard the animals while they sleep.

When the farmer and his wife arrived to pick out their puppy, they were surrounded with many puppies to choose from.

The decision was very difficult, but they fell in love with one little fellow.

Most Great Pyrenees dogs are white. But some of them can have grey, black, or tan markings on them. These markings are called badger marks.

The puppy they fell in love with had badger markings on his face and ears. He had dark grey markings on both ears, and he looked like he had a dark grey, almost black patch over his left eye.

The farmer and his wife were so excited to bring their new puppy home and introduce him to all the other animals on the farm!

There were already two older Great Pyrenees dogs on the farm, and they would train him on how to do his job.

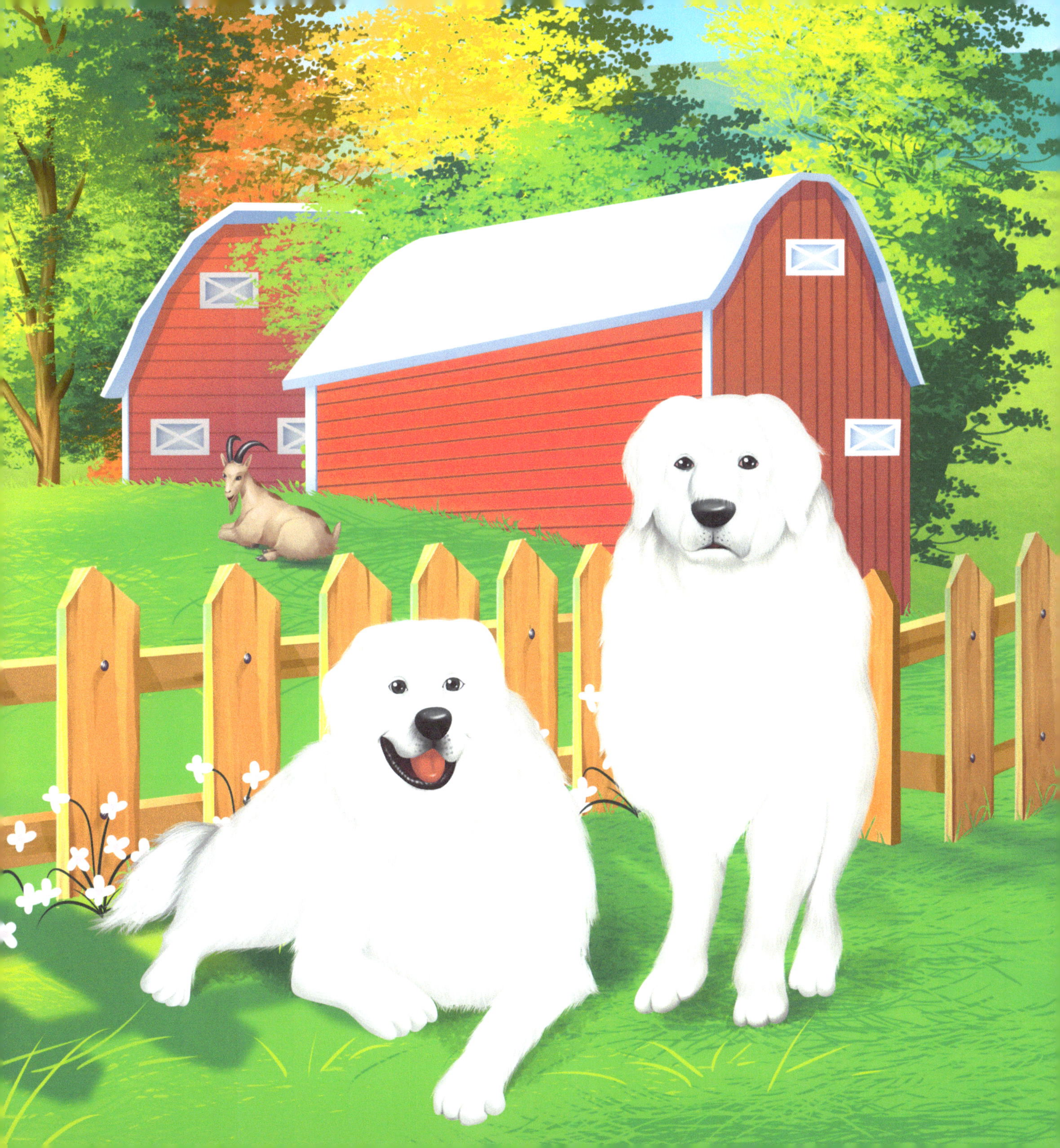

On their drive home, the farmer and his wife were trying to decide what his name would be. What would they call him? Naming a puppy can be very difficult!

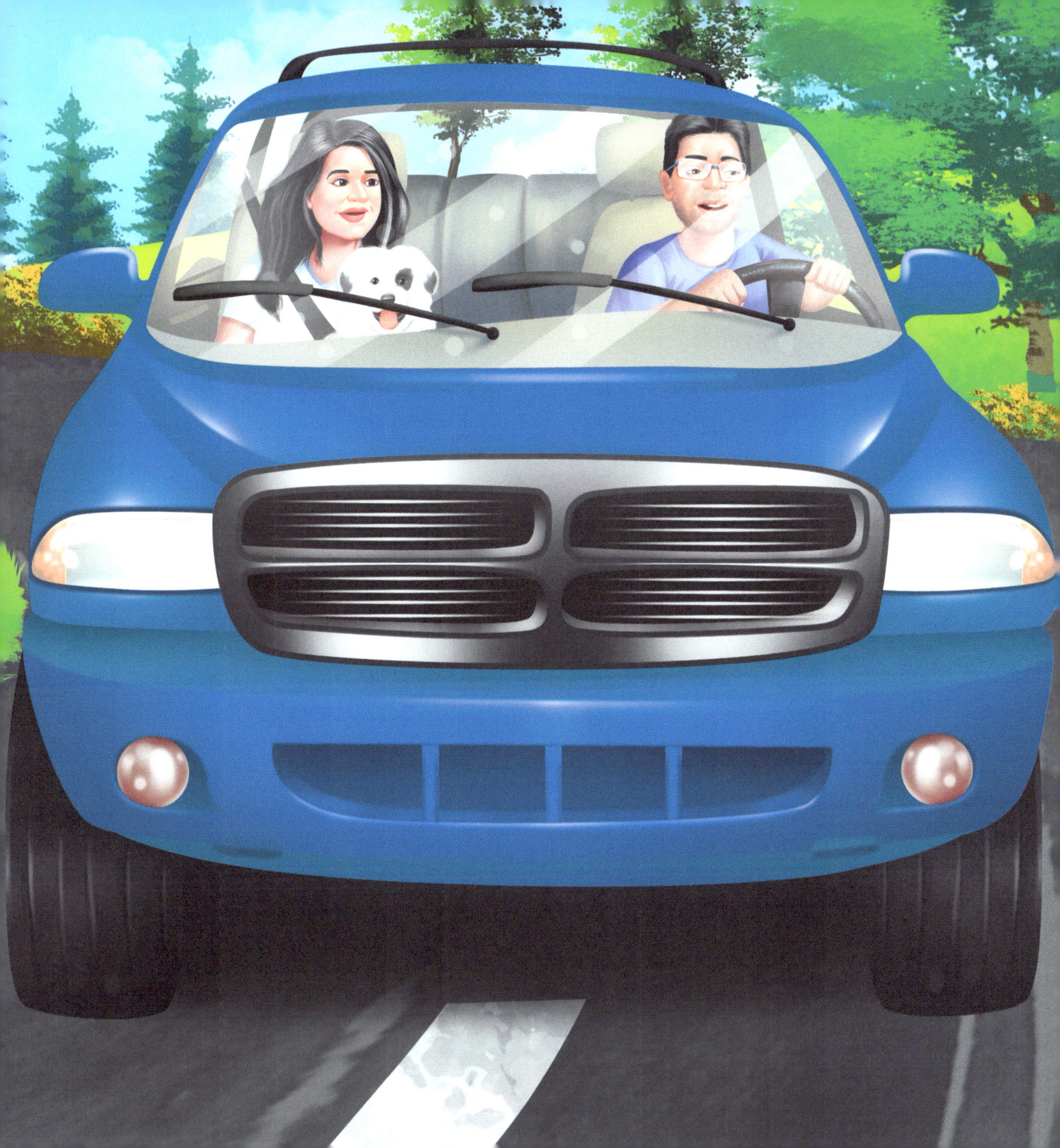

Should we call him Fred? Or Rover? Or ...
"Wait," said the farmer. "Let's call him Rooster!"

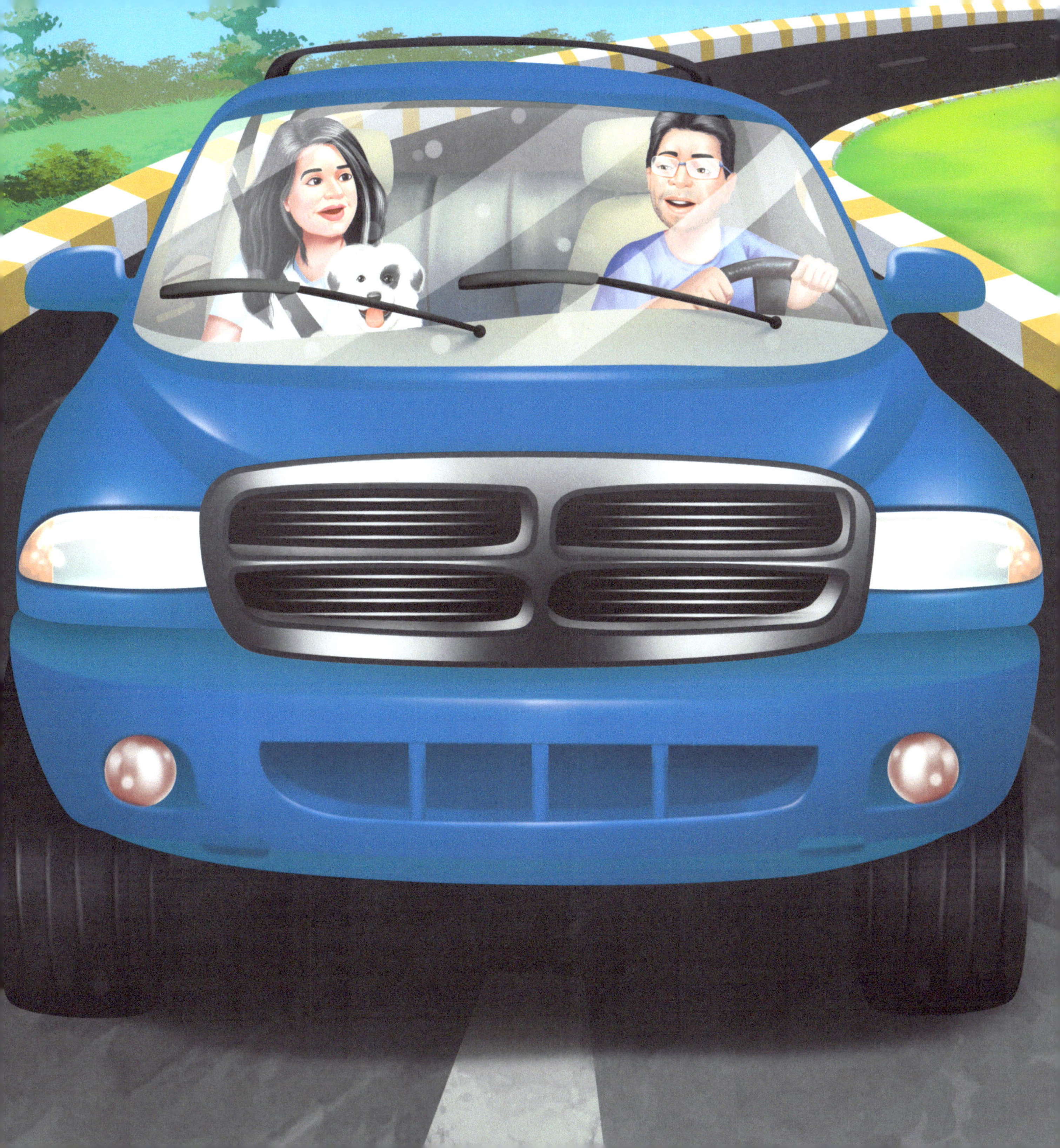

Laughing loudly, the farmer's wife asked: "Why on earth would you name a dog Rooster"?

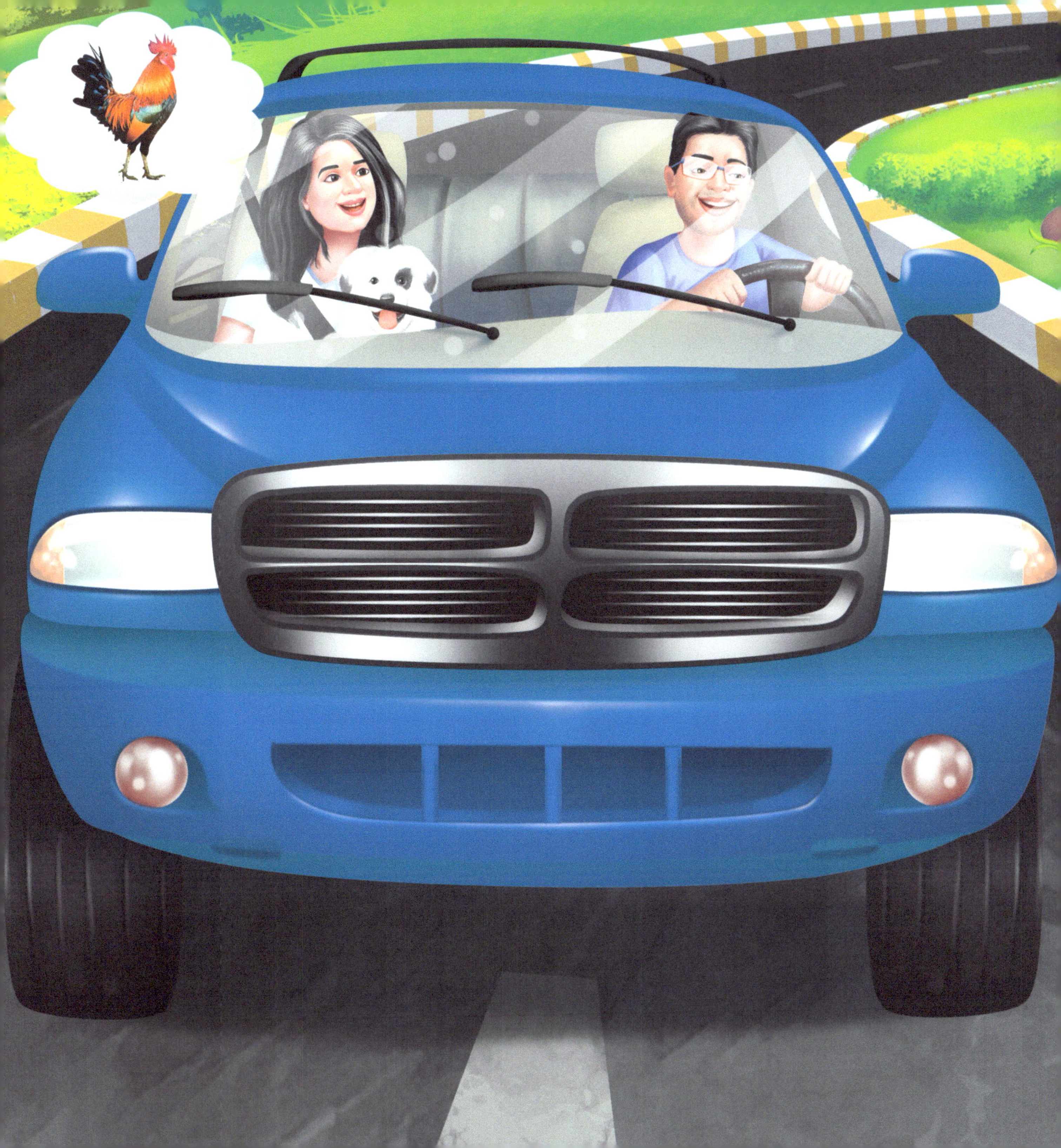

The farmer explained that he once watched an old western movie where a cowboy with a black patch over his eye was called Rooster by the town's people. He was a strong cowboy that protected the people in the town.

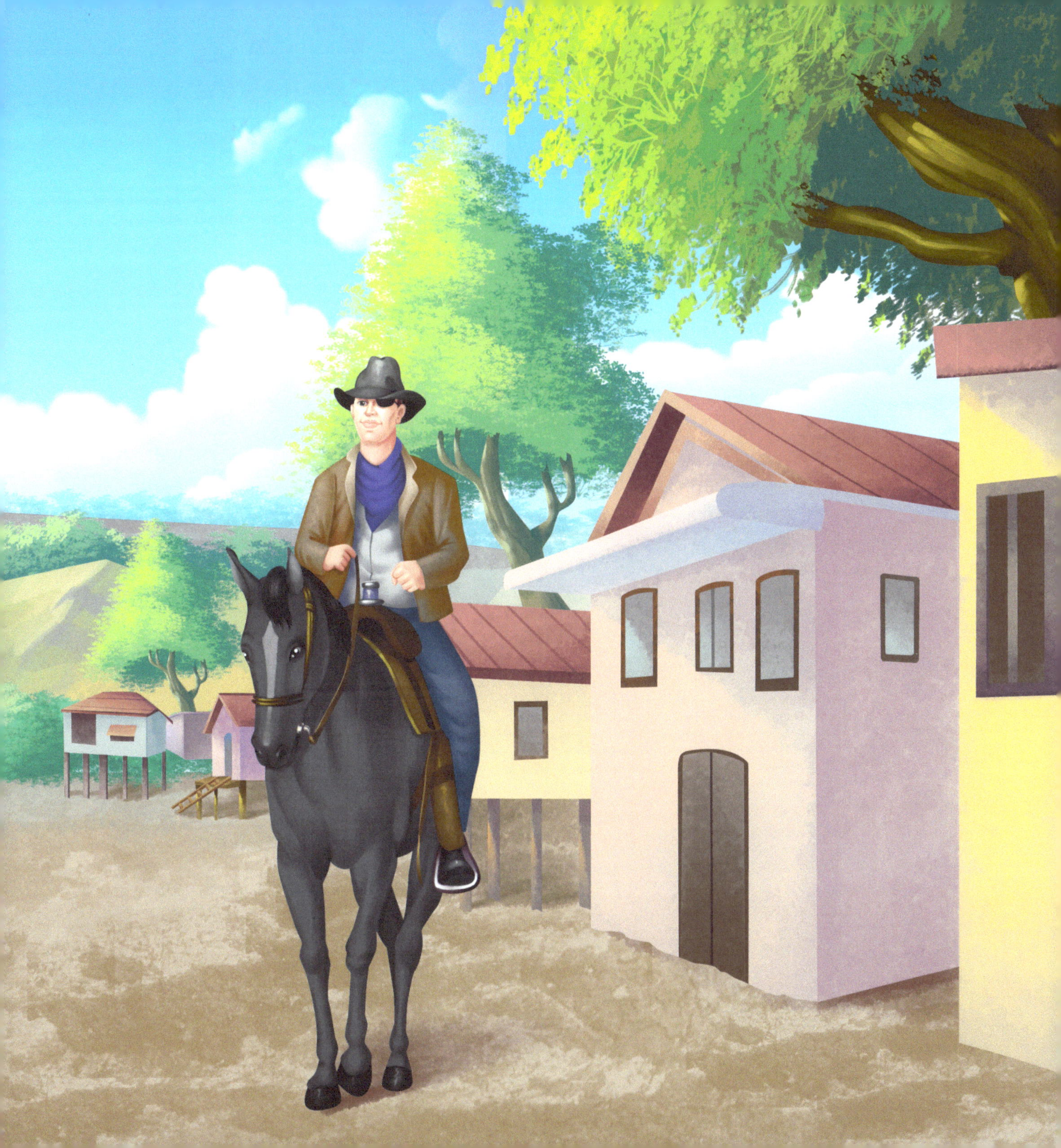

Like the cowboy, the puppy had a patch over his eye. Also, like the cowboy, the puppy would be a strong protector. And that is how Rooster got his name.

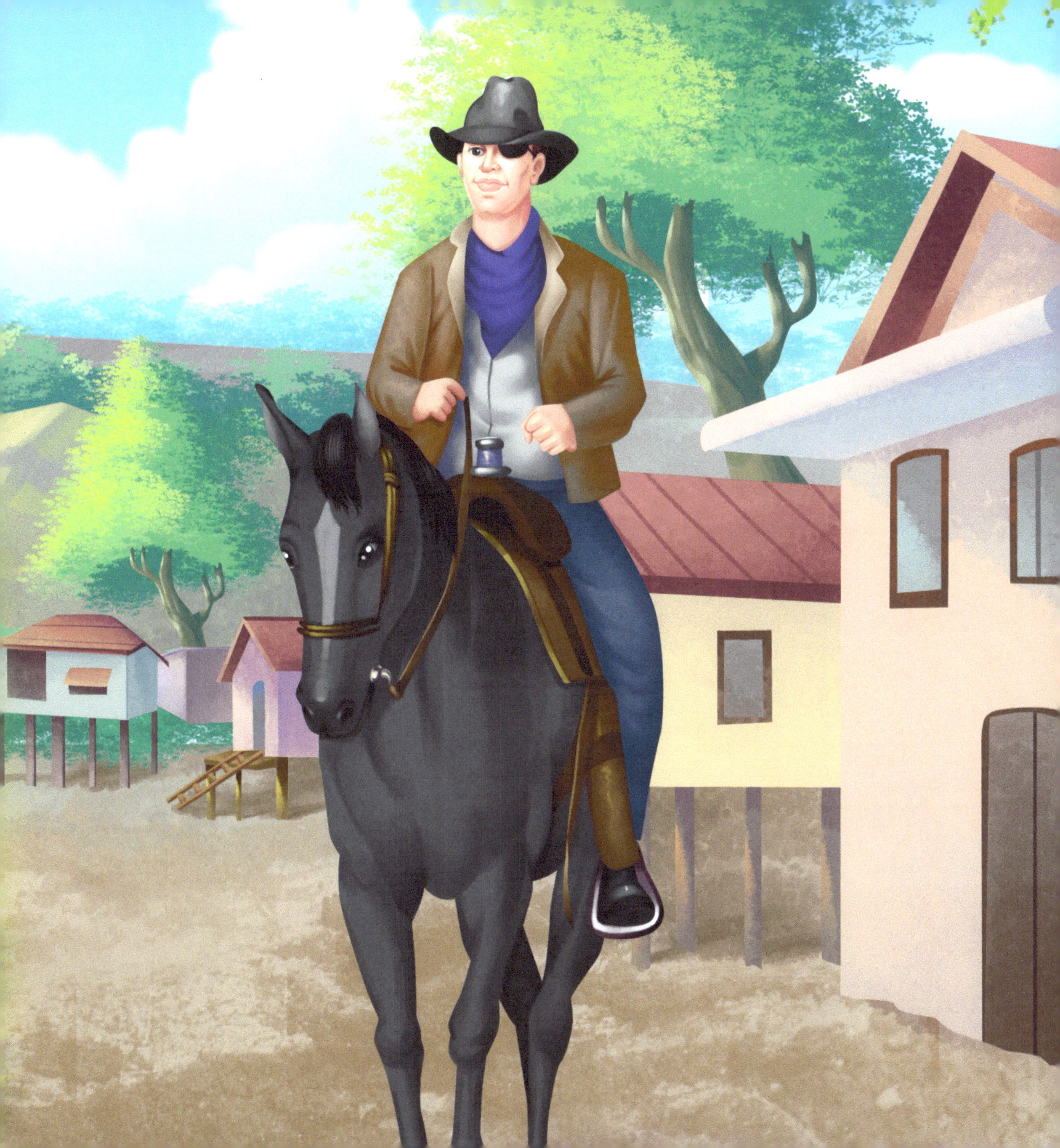

As Rooster grew, his badger marks moved. This is very common with Great Pyrenees dogs. The badger markings can sometimes disappear entirely.

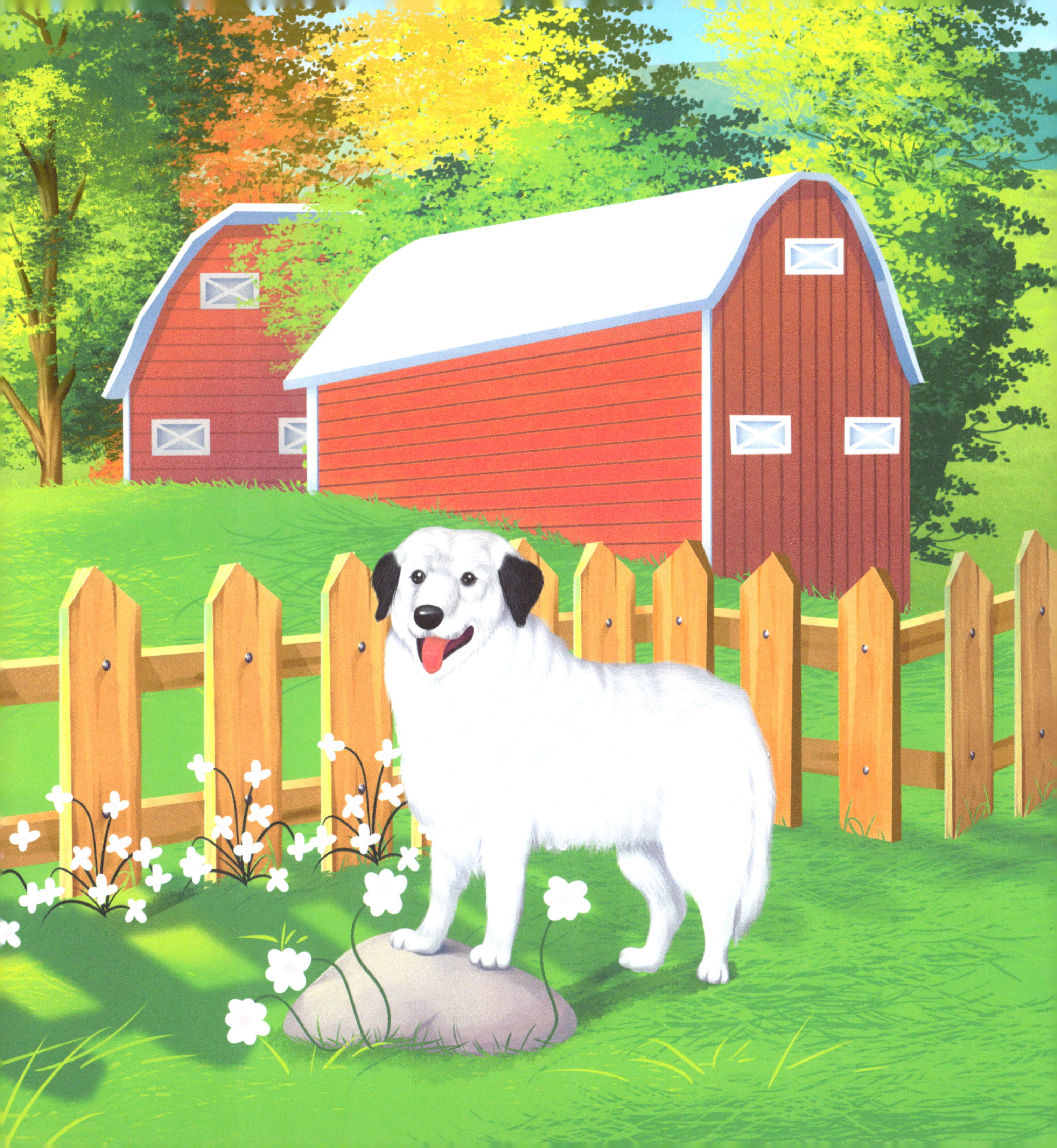

Rooster's badger markings moved back on his face and remained on his ears.

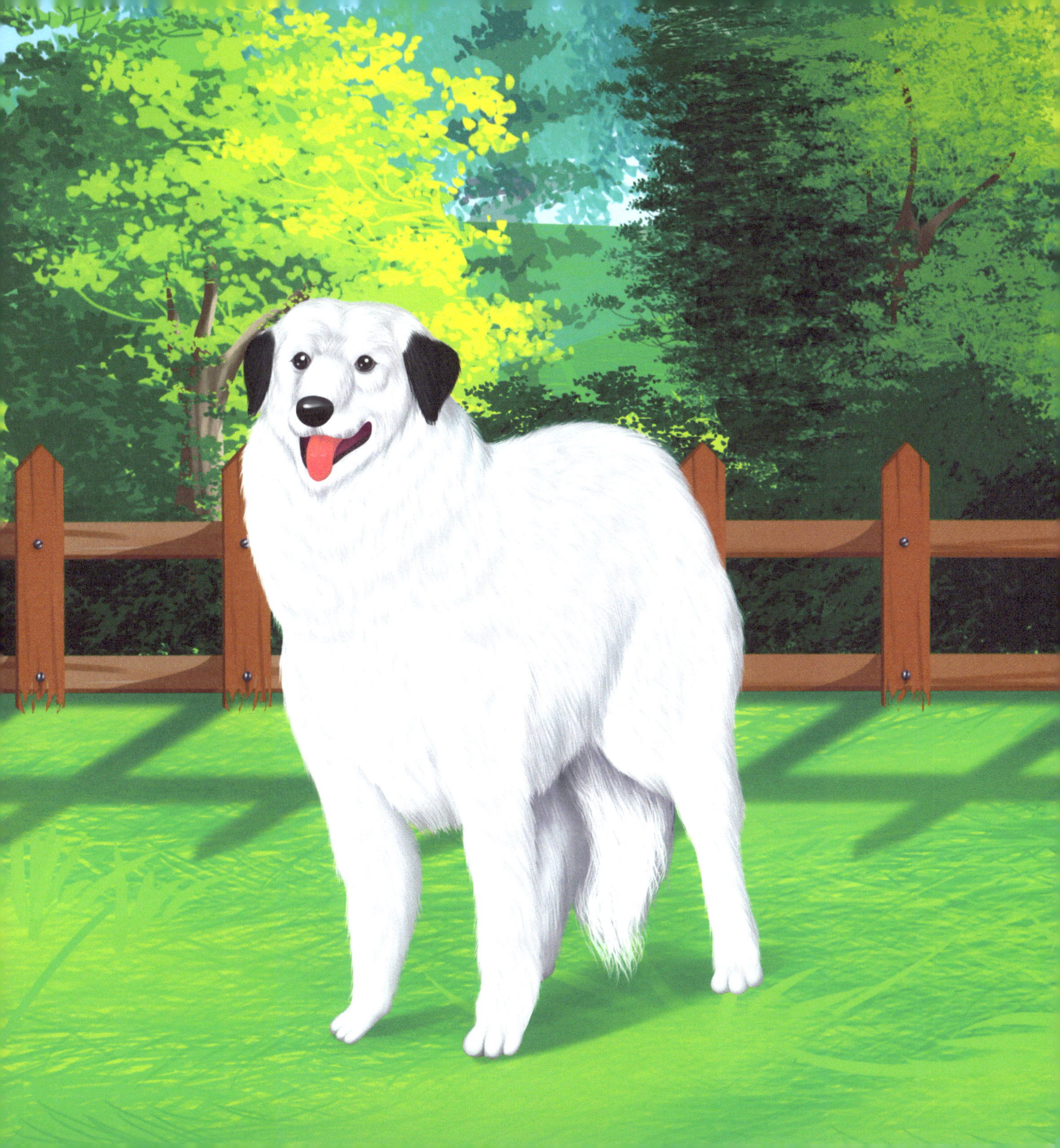

Rooster grew up and with the proper training from the older Pyrenees dogs on the farm, he became a great protector at Horseshoe Ridge Farms! He protected many animals on the farm!

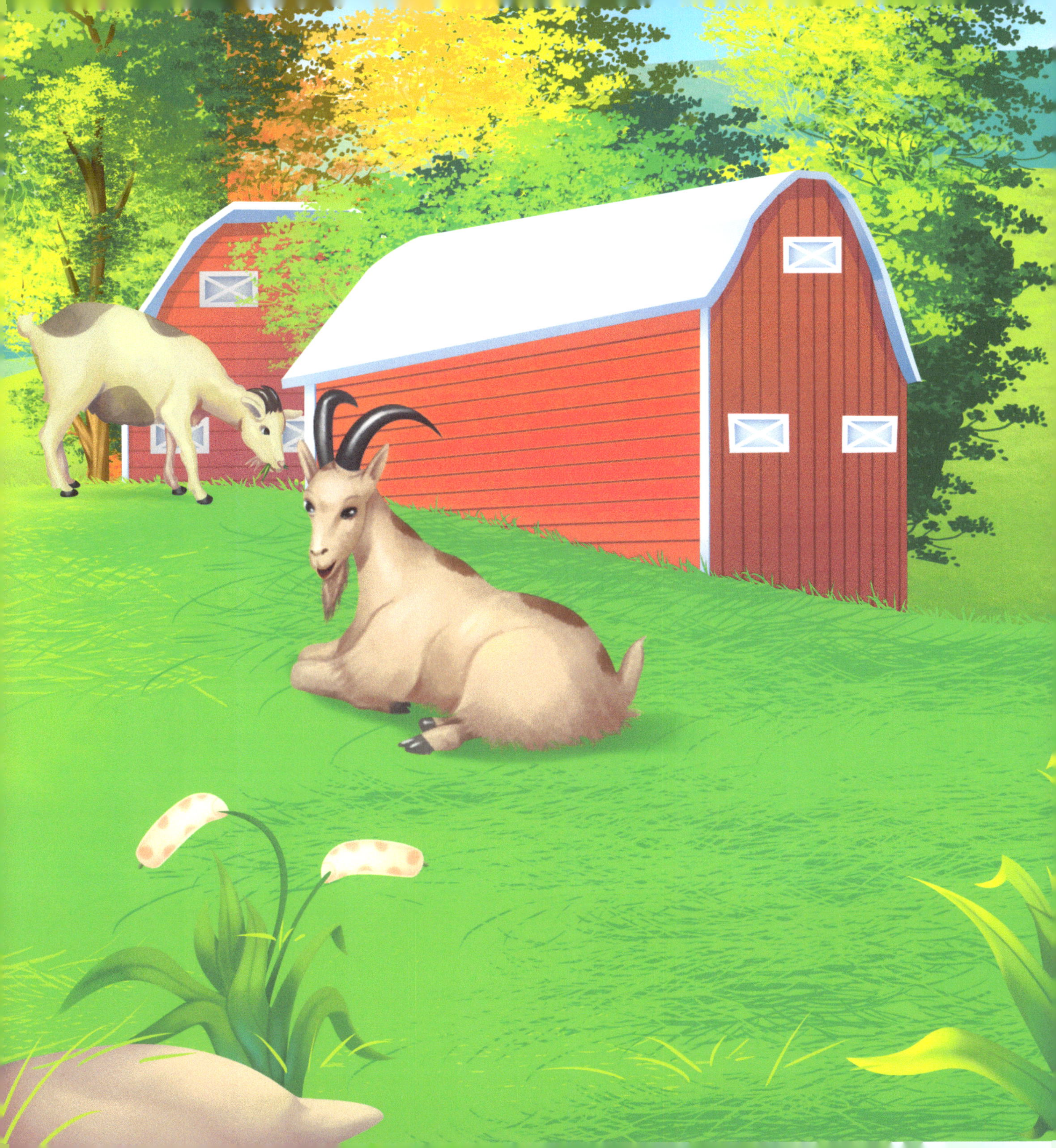

Rooster even protected the Farmer's wife and their grandchildren! He stayed very close to them as they roamed the pastures checking on the animals!

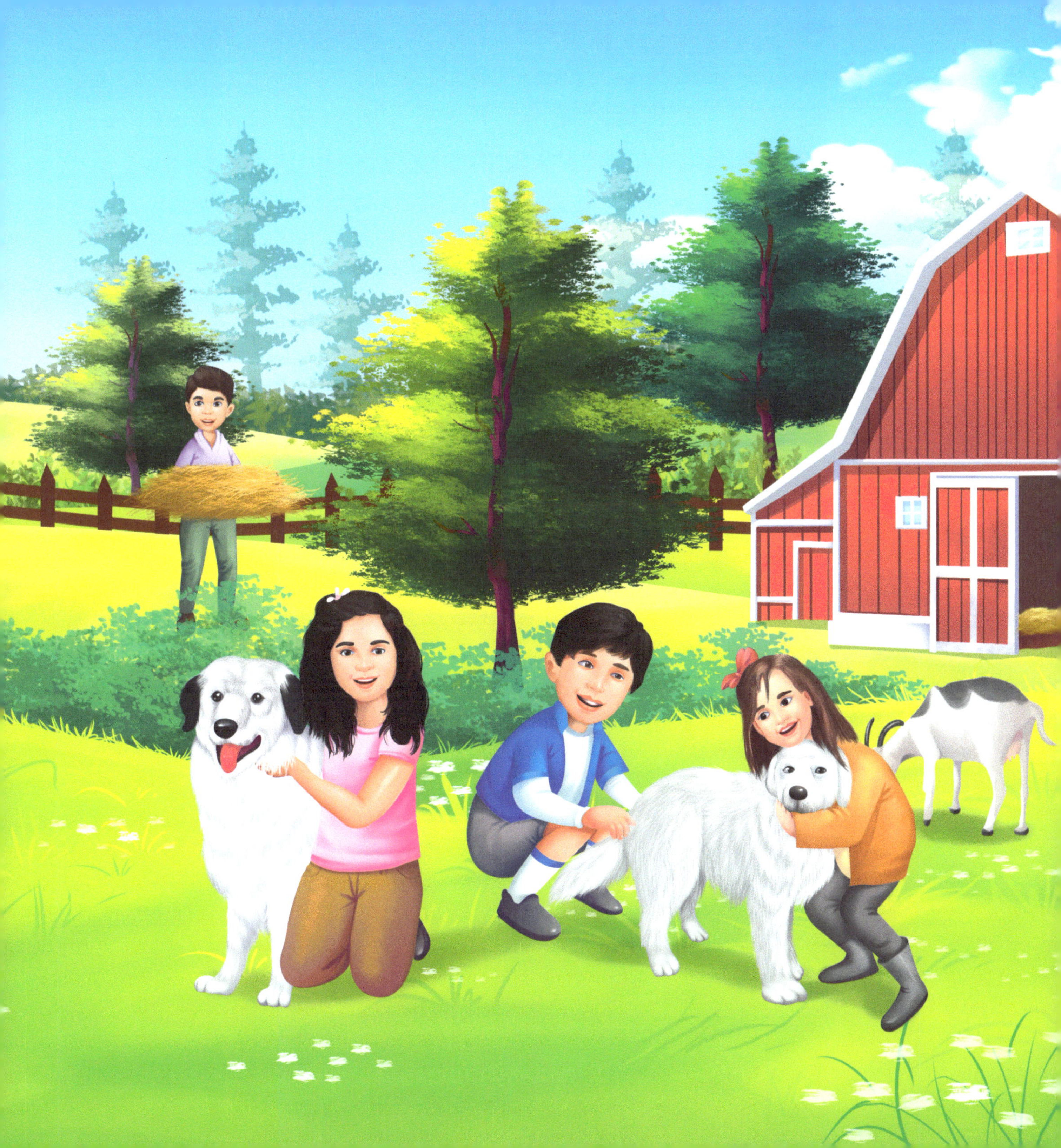

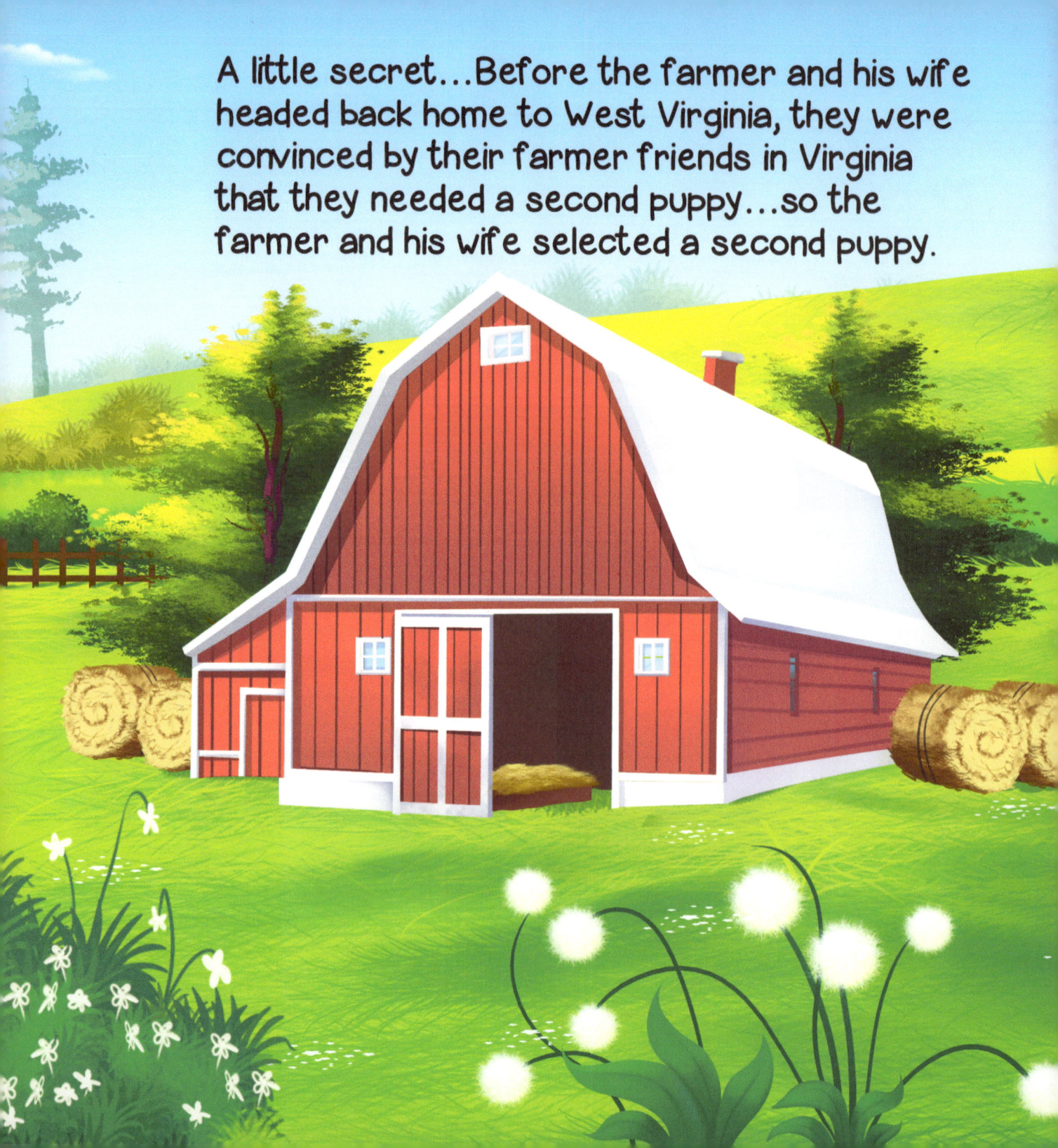

A little secret…Before the farmer and his wife headed back home to West Virginia, they were convinced by their farmer friends in Virginia that they needed a second puppy…so the farmer and his wife selected a second puppy.

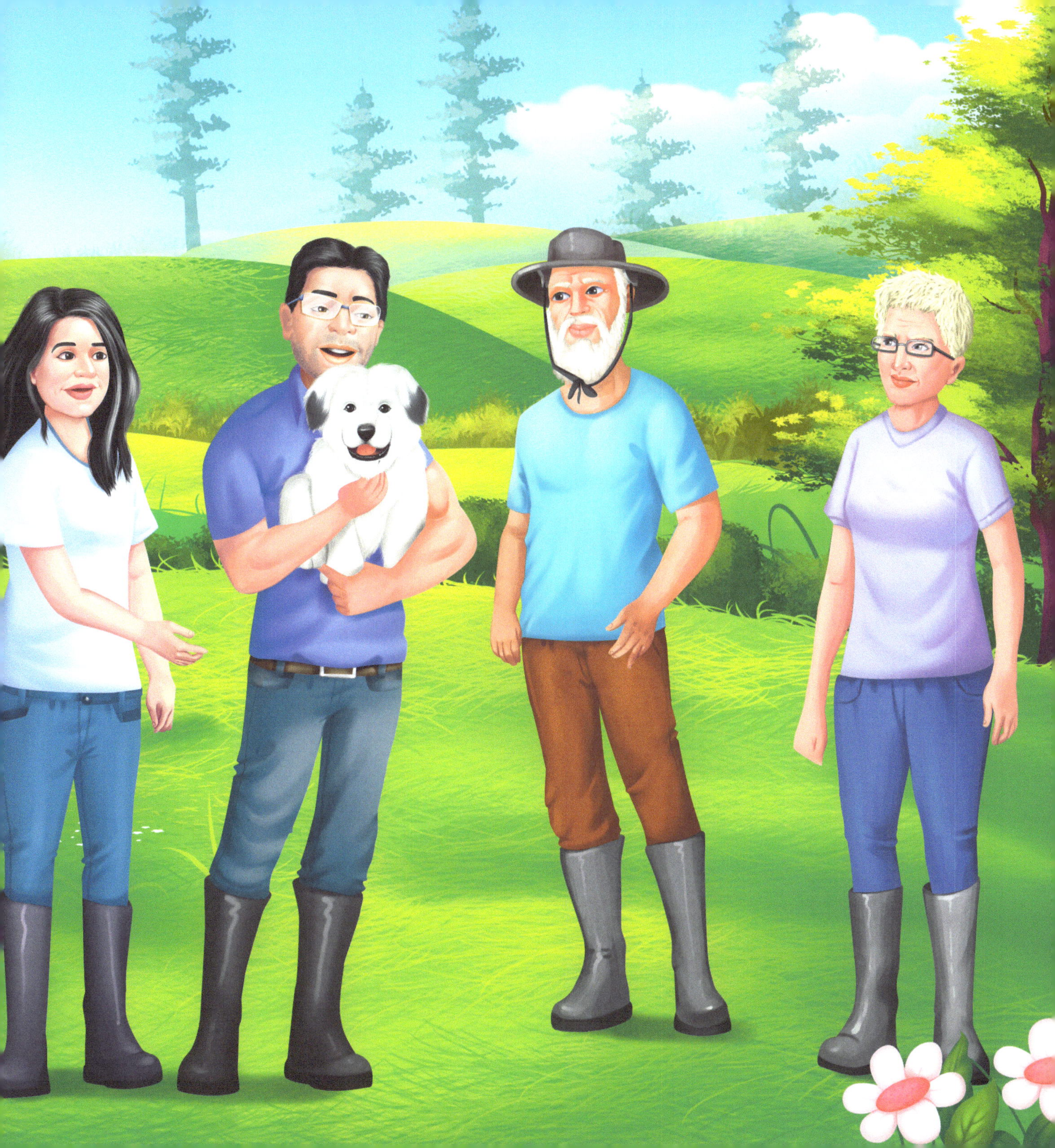

You will have to read the next book in the series so you can read all about the second puppy! Find out how brave she and Rooster were when they worked together to protect the livestock!

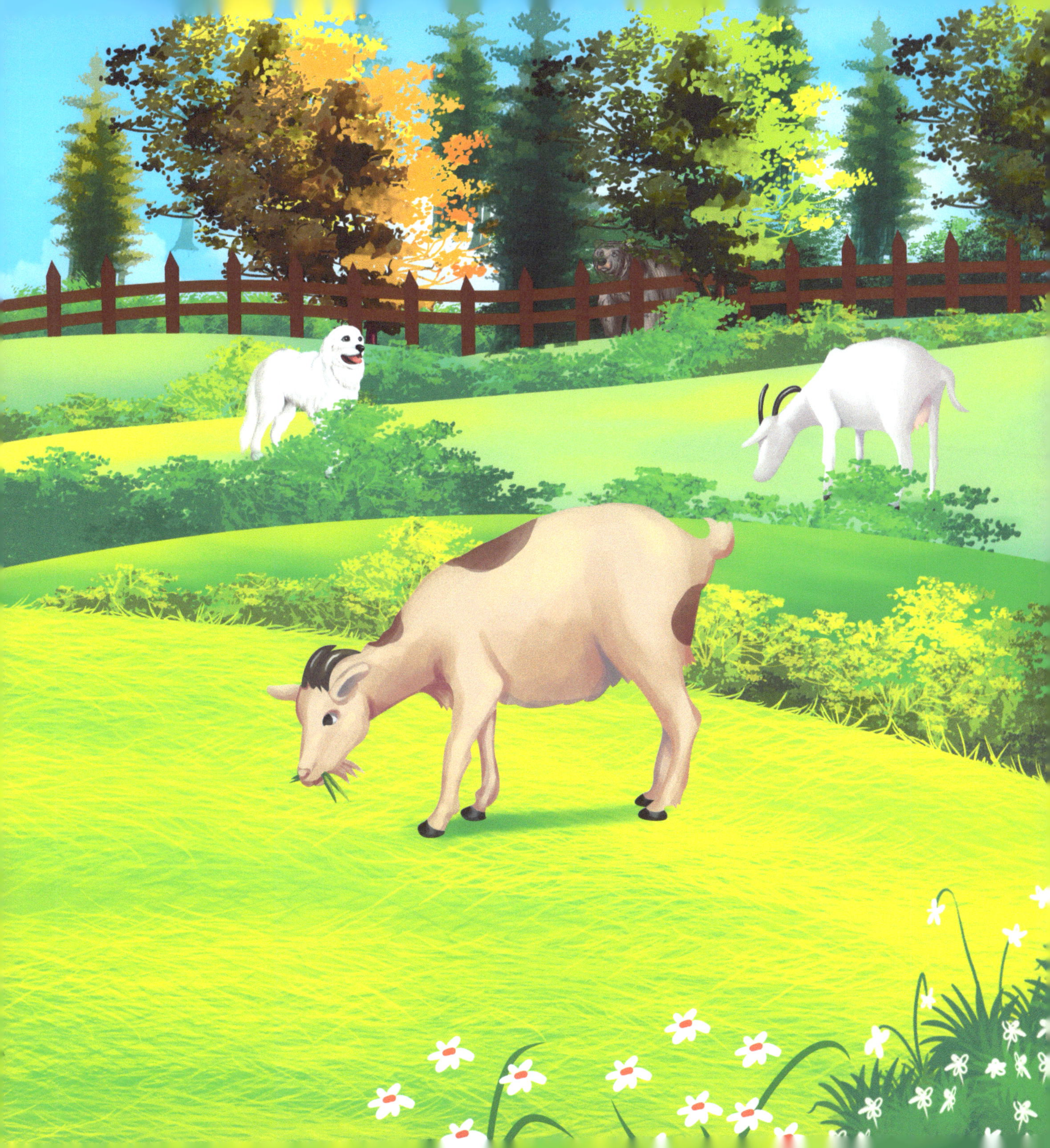

THE END

Until the Next Farm Adventure!

ABOUT THE AUTHOR

Lucy M. Johnson is the Farmers' wife. Lucy was born and raised in Albuquerque, New Mexico. At age 19, Lucy decided she needed a new adventure, so she joined the United States Air Force (USAF) and that is where her life would change forever. On her way to her first duty station in sunny Spain, Lucy met a handsome young man who was also heading to Spain. This young man changed her life. Lucy and Rick (the Farmer) were married in 1985 and were blessed with three wonderful children and eight beautiful grandchildren.

During her distinguished USAF career, Lucy served as a Logistician, Academic Instructor, and Network System Administrator. While in the USAF, she earned a bachelor's degree in human resource management, and a dual master's degree in human resource development and computer resources and information technology. After retiring from the Air Force, Lucy went back to school and completed her PhD in organization and management with a concentration in emotional intelligence.

Lucy and Rick (also retired USAF) settled in WV, the Farmers' home state. They built a home and Rick began building Horseshoe Ridge Farms while Lucy continued working on various information technology contracts. In 2021, Lucy and Rick added to the adventures by opening Horseshoe Ridge Farms AirBnB where they host guests on the farm.

It is here, on the farm, that all the adventures take place, all the animals roam freely on the beautiful hills of WV. The farm is Lucy's happy place where she lives the adventures and draws inspiration to write and share her adventures with others. Lucy has always said: "I love people more than computers" and she hopes to bring smiles to many faces with her writings.

VISIT US

HORSESHOE RIDGE FARMS
& AirBnB

Website Link:
www.horseshoeridgefarms.com

AirBnB Link:
https://www.airbnb.com/rooms/31174685?s=3

Amazon Author Page:
https://www.amazon.com/author/lucymjohnson

Milton Keynes UK
Ingram Content Group UK Ltd.
UKHW051855280424
441853UK00003B/7